THE COMPLETE LIBRARY SKILLS
Kindergarten, First Grade & Second Grade

by
Linda Turrell

Cover and inside illustrations by
Darcy Myers

Publishers
T.S. Denison & Company, Inc.
Minneapolis, Minnesota 55431

Standard Book Number:513-02209-0
The Complete Library Skills – Kindergarten, Grade One, Grade Two
Copyright © 1994 by T.S. Denison & Company, Inc.
9601 Newton Avenue South
Minneapolis, Minnesota 55431

Printed in the USA

CONTENTS

SECOND GRADE

KINDERGARTEN

The library skills curriculum for kindergarten children will lay the foundation for all the elementary years to come. During this special first year of school, kindergartners will learn how to properly care for a book, where picture books are located in the library, how to use a shelf marker, how to check out a book, the importance of returning a book on time, and they'll develop a love of books.

A visit to the library should be an experience that young children look forward to. They will quickly learn that the librarian/media center specialist is a person who can provide them with a wealth of information in a place where their imaginations can soar!

Begin your school year by teaching the children specific library citizenship rules. These rules will help the children better understand the library, and assist them in developing the self-confidence they will need when looking for books and for asking questions.

CONTENTS

CARING FOR A BOOK

Caring for a book is a responsibility that needs to be taught. Young children are often hard on books and materials without realizing that their carelessness can cause damage. Here are some ideas that will assist you in teaching young children how to care for a book.

- **Brainstorm** with the children all their ideas about how one should care for a book. Children very often have excellent ideas about proper book care.

- **Book bags** are an excellent habit to instill in young children for use on library day. Discuss with the children how the book bag (or back pack) will protect the book when they carry it to and from school.

- **Read the children the story of,** *Mr. Wiggle's Book,* written by Paula Craig and published by T.S. Denison. It is a wonderful story about a little book worm who lives in a book that has been damaged by careless children. At the end of the story Mr. Wiggle is glad that the listeners of the story know how to care for a book.

- **Book patrol badges** made from cardboard and covered with foil are a project that the children can wear as they investigate and look for books in the library that need repair. Discuss the importance of telling the librarian when a book is damaged. Damaged books must be repaired by the librarian.

- Use the reproducible coloring book, *I Know How To Take Care Of A Book (The Story of Leo, the Library Mouse),* found on pages 7 to 11. Read the book to the class and discuss the book care rules. The children may take the book home to share with their parents. Purchase a stuffed animal mouse or ask parents to donate a mouse that could be used as the kindergarten library mascot. Let your "Leo" join the class at storytime.

- Praise the children for properly caring for books. Reproducible **Bookmark Awards** (page 12), **Library Citizenship Poster** (pages 16 & 17), and **Library Awards** (page 21) are provided for you.

I Know How To Take Care Of A Book

(The Story of "Leo, the Library Mouse")

A "Read-At-Home" Book

Colored by _____

Hi! My name is Leo, the Library Mouse. I love the library and I love books! I know how to take good care of books. Read and color my book and you will know how to take good care of books too!

1

Clean hands keep books clean.
I always make sure that my hands
are clean before I touch a book.
Remember to wash off all the
cheese, peanut butter and jelly.

2

I love artwork, but I would *never write, scribble, glue,
or cut the pages of a book.* When I want to make art,
I use paper, not the pages of a book.

3

Sometimes I do not finish looking at a book in one setting. *I mark my place with a bookmark,* or with a scrap of paper. I would never fold the page of a book to mark my place.

In some books I have a favorite picture that I like to find over and over again. I mark my favorite picture with a bookmark too!

4

Turning a page too fast or the wrong way can cause the page to rip! Oh dear! *I turn the page using the top corner of the page.* When I do this, the page turns easily and I cannot rip it!

5

I love to bring home library books. *I always remember to bring a book bag,* back pack, or plastic bag to carry home my books. If I drop my books or if it rains, the books will be safe in my bag.

6

When I get my books home I am careful that I keep them in a safe place. I have a baby sister who does not know how to take care of books. I also have a pet ant that likes to chew my books. I put my books on a table or bookshelf so I know that my books are safe.

7

When I have finished looking at my books *I remember to bring them back to the library on time.* It is important to bring your library books back on time because other children want to look at them too!

8

Leo, the Library Mouse wants us to remember these important rules:

1. Clean hands keep books clean.
2. Never write, scribble, glue, or cut the pages of a book.
3. Mark your place in a book with a bookmark, not by folding the page of a book.
4. Turn the page by using the top corner.
5. Always carry your books in some type of book bag.
6. Keep your books in a safe place at home, where little brothers, sisters, or pets cannot bother them.
7. Remember to return your books to the library on time.

9

LIBRARY CITIZENSHIP BOOKMARKS

Reproduce the bookmarks. Use as rewards or as a springboard for a lesson about library citizenship.

<u>   </u>
child's name

was a good listener at library story time!

Have you ever heard the expression, *"Quiet as a mouse?"* In our library you may talk – but not too loud!

The librarian wants you to ask questions and talk about the books you are looking at. Just remember to speak in an "inside voice."

Many good friends can be found in a book. Who are some of your favorite characters?

DO YOU KNOW HOW TO TAKE CARE OF A BOOK?

NAME _____

Color the picture that shows how you should carry your books to school.	
Color the picture that shows a safe place to keep your books at home.	
Color the book that someone took good care of.	
Color the mouse that is ready to touch a book.	

Leo, the Library Mouse needs to return his books to the library today! Help him find the way through the maze so he can get his books back to the library on time!

Many books are kept in the library in ABC order.
Practice putting the alphabet in order by connecting the dots.
Do you know who this is?

LIBRARY CITIZENSHIP

Treat books with respect.

You may talk in the library, but use an inside voice.

Remember to sign out your books properly.

Always return library books on time.

Carry your books to and from the library in a book bag.

If you discover a damaged book, give it to the librarian. Library books are mended with special materials.

Remember to share books with your friends.

Stories are fun to hear. Be a good listener.

Turn the pages of a book from the top corner.

Be considerate of others.

Librarians love to help! Ask questions.

SHELF MARKER

Explain to the children that picture books live in the library – each in it's own special place or house. It is important to put a book back in its proper house. When you take a book off a shelf use a shelf marker to place in the spot where the book has been removed.

Reproduce this shelf marker on construction paper. Have the children color. Laminate for durability.

The shelf markers made by the children are kept in the library and used when they come to the library and look for books. At the end of the year you may send them home with the children.

Dear Parents,

Today your kindergartner brought home a book from the school library for the first time. This is an exciting moment for a young child. It is a "grown-up" feeling being allowed to choose a book, bring it home, and have the personal responsibility of properly caring for the book.

We have spent time at school discussing library citizenship and how to take care of a book. Although the children have learned many library rules and considerations they will need your help with reminders.

Mark on your calendar (possibly taped on the refrigerator, at eye-level for your child) your child's assigned library day. This day is _____, and is the day that books should be returned to school.

Please see that your child carries his/her library books to school in a book bag or backpack. Carrying books in some sort of bag is easier for a small child and will help keep the books protected.

Learning to read for a young child is a thrilling experience. You can foster this attitude by reading to your child, and encouraging your child to look at and enjoy books. This is a memorable experience for both parents and children.

Thank you for your assistance,

School Librarian

CHECKING OUT BOOKS — CARD SIGNING

Children should be allowed to sign library check-out cards as soon as possible. The following large library card can be made into a transparency and used on an overhead projector. Children love to practice signing their names and using an overhead projector makes it even more fun. The card may also be reproduced for individual practice.

Stress the importance of only using one line of the card.

Se		
Author	Dr. Seuss	
Title	The Cat In The Hat	

Date Due	Borrower's Name	Room Number

RETURN REMINDERS/ AWARDS

Young children love earning awards. Two of these awards may be used to reward a child for returning his/her library books on time. The other award is a reminder that library day is coming up and that the books will be due soon.

STORYTELLING IDEAS

One of the most special times of the day for a young child is "storytime." During this time you can create an educational experience that is a lot of fun and one that will motivate children to want to explore books.

BENEFITS OF STORYTELLING

1. We all hope that children will enter school with a beginning knowledge and appreciation of books, but unfortunately this is not always true. There are many young children who start school and have not been afforded the opportunity of having books in their environment. The school library and the stories told at school may be a child's first introduction to the world of books.

2. The story hour and the books you choose to read or "tell" help to teach an appreciation of literature.

3. Storytelling is one of the most effective means of increasing language development in the young child. Not only are listening skills increased, but expressive vocabulary begins to soar when storytelling is incorporated into a child's daily life.

4. Storytime is an excellent tool for increasing listening or "paying attention" skills.

5. Cultural traditions of people can be taught through storytelling.

6. Storytelling can also be used to teach and reinforce academic subjects such as reading, math, science, geography, etc.

7. ... And of course, storytelling will entertain, amuse and delight young children!

THE "HOW-TO-PREPARE" FOR STORYTELLING or 'THE DO'S"

1. Read the story through once, just for your own enjoyment.

2. Read it again for the sequence of events and pay special attention to the outline of the plot.

3. Choose some "high" words — colorful words — to give flavor to your story.

4. Find some "key phrases" like "Fee-fi-fo-fum," "Mirror, mirror on the wall," or "I'll huff and puff and blow your house down." When key phrases are used in the story, ask the children to say those key phrases with you.

5. Practice telling the story. Read it over several times.

6. The ending is very important. Strive to retain the mood of your story. If it is joyous use a lifting voice; if it is serious, use a sober tone.

7. Help the children visualize the story as you go along, and bring the characters alive for them. If a child misbehaves or is inattentive, look him right in the eye and you will bring his/her attention back to you. Don't interrupt the story by stopping to correct behavior. Keep telling the story and move next to the child who seems to need some attention. Look at all the children as you tell a story, and try to include all of them.

SOME DO NOT'S

Do not speak too fast or overly dramatic. Be cautious that you do not speak down to the children. Don't explain in too much detail, you might lose their attention by explaining too much. And finally, do not keep the children beyond their attention span, or by telling too many stories in one setting. No matter how long they beg for more, leave them wanting more.

GRADE ONE

The first grade child is ready to begin accepting some responsibility for following the accepted procedures in the library, such as signing his/her own book cards, taking proper care of books, and in making book selections. Since first graders are learning to read, it will become important that they are able to select books that they can read independently. Offer guidance and provide an area of the library where they can find books that are appropriate for their reading level. Children at this age are also ready to be introduced to books by an author, illustrator, or by topic. Experiences with books should create a continuous desire to learn to read for enjoyment and information.

CONTENTS

Dear Parents,

The most thrilling part of first grade is learning to read. It is a magical experience for a young child. This thrill needs to be shared and "shown-off."

When your child brings home a book from the library, or with the books that you may have at your home, sit with your child as he/she reads and really listen. Help your child with proper names, uncommon words, or words that may be difficult to sound out.

Discuss the story as you are reading or when you are finished. "What part of the story did you like best?" "Who was your favorite character?" "Did you like the way the story ended?" "Can you think of another way the story might have ended?" "What was your favorite picture in the book?" There are so many questions that can be asked that will help your child remember what they have read, and will provide a better understanding of the story.

In first grade, we expect that the children will begin taking more responsibility for caring for their library books, and in making their own book selections. Your child's library day is _____. Although children at this age want to be more independent, they will still need your reminders about returning library books on time. Post library day on your refrigerator and encourage your child to try and remember when to return books.

I look forward to an exciting year with all the "eager-to-read" first graders.

School Librarian

HOW TO PUT BOOKS ON A SHELF

When you are looking at books in the library it is important to put the books back on the shelves properly. Books should stand straight and tall on the book shelves.

Look at the book shelf on this paper. Some of the books on the shelves are not standing properly. Color the books that have been put on the shelves the correct way.

SHELF MARKER

Look at this big book shelf. Cut the small shelf markers and glue them on the shelves where a shelf marker should be.

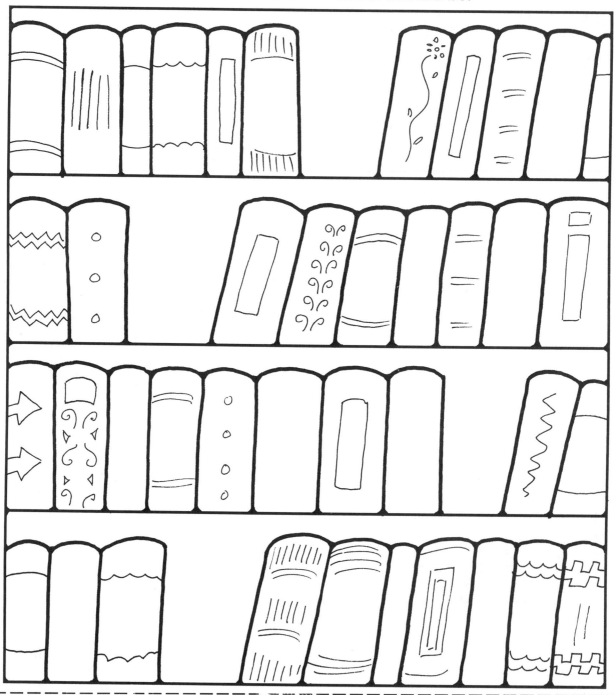

cut and paste

 Shelf Marker **Shelf Marker**

 Shelf Marker **Shelf Marker**

BOOKS ARE PUT IN "ABC" ORDER

Books are organized in the library in alphabetical or "ABC" order. Let's practice the alphabet!

LEARNING TO PUT
BOOKS IN "ABC" ORDER

The library has many books. Library books are put on the shelves
in "ABC" order. Can you put these books back in "ABC" order?
Draw a line from the book to its correct place on the shelf.

NAME _____

LEARNING TO PUT BOOKS IN "ABC" ORDER

The book shelves are empty! Ten books need to be put away. Cut out the books and glue them on the book shelf in "ABC" order.

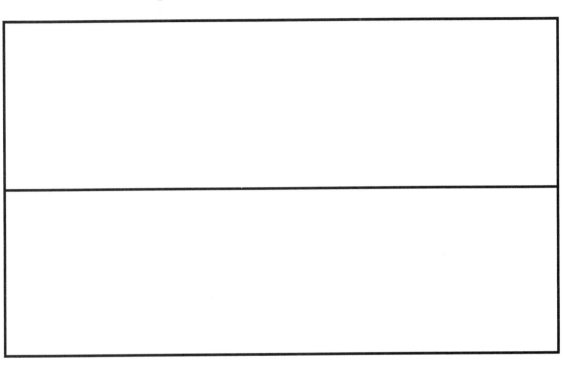

FILL IN MISSING BOOKS   NAME _____

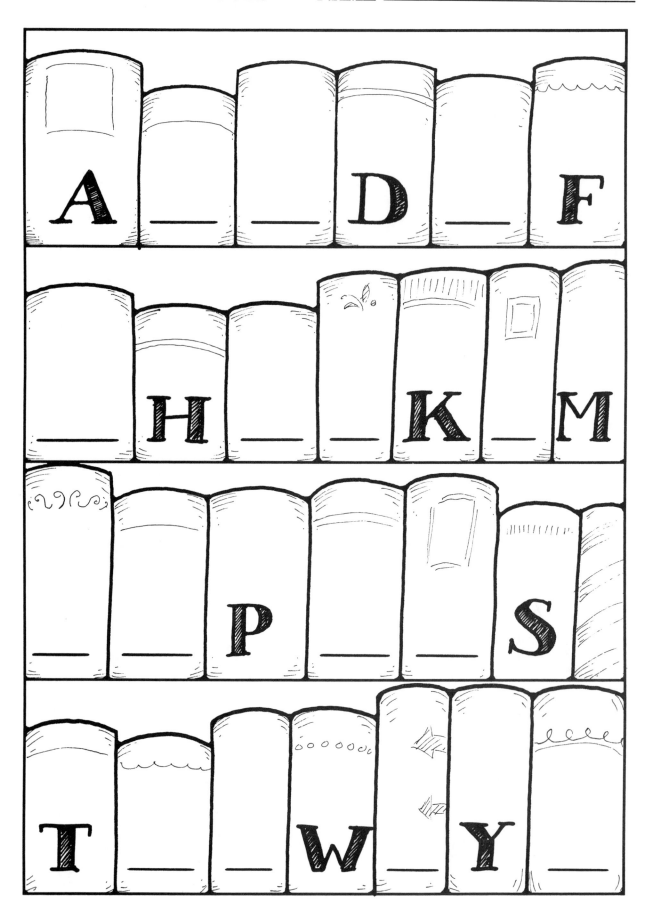

A __ __ D __ F

__ H __ __ K __ M

__ __ P __ __ S __

T __ __ W __ Y __

WHICH BOOK COMES NEXT?

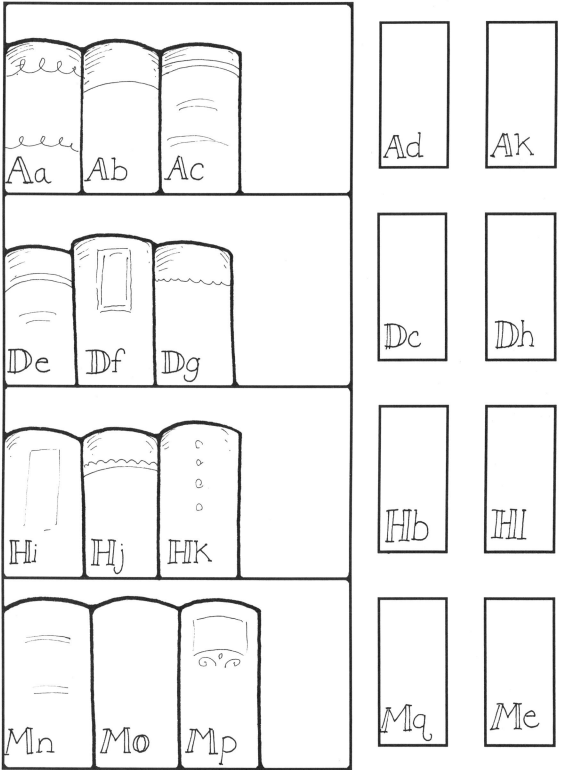

Cut out the correct book and paste in on the shelf.

NAME _____

LET'S LOOK AT "2" LETTERS

Put these books back in "ABC" order using two letters.
Draw a line matching the books.
Color the book shelf that is in "ABC" order.

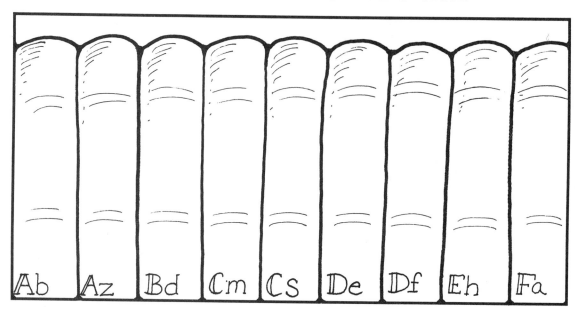

Ab Az Bd Cm Cs De Df Eh Fa

Cm Fa Ab Df Eh Bd Az De Cs

NAME _____

LET'S LOOK AT "2" LETTERS

Color the book that should come next in each of the book shelves.
Look carefully at both the letters on each book.

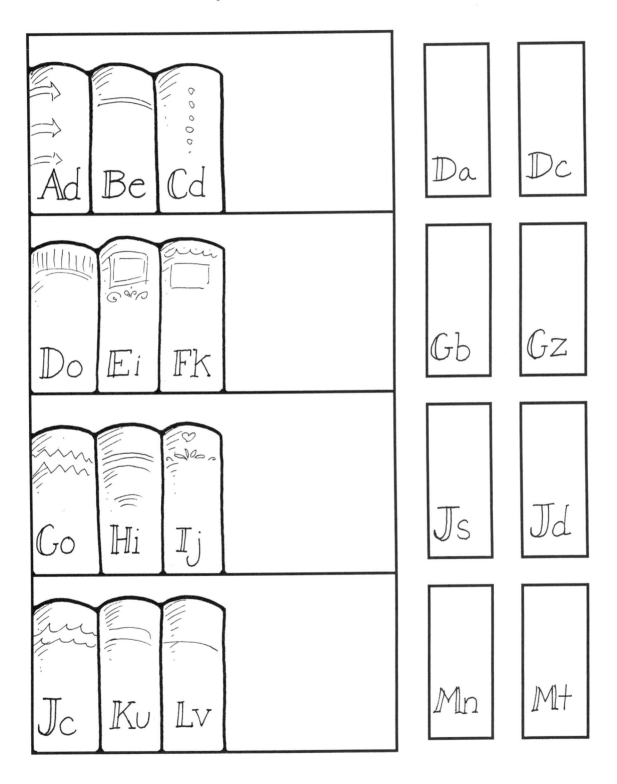

BORROWING LIBRARY BOOKS

Children should learn to feel that checking out a book from the library is a responsibility. When children take out books from the library they are promising to be good citizens and that they will take good care of the book they have checked out.

Provide the children with some practice in properly signing out a book from the library. Encourage the children to use the first available line on the card. Here are some cards for practice.

E		
W		
Author	Ward	
Title	The Biggest Bear	

DATE DUE	BORROWER'S NAME	ROOM
Sept. 24	Suzi Brown	101

DATE DUE	BORROWER'S NAME	ROOM
Oct. 1	Tim Jones	402
Jan. 2	Zach Smith	21

DATE DUE	BORROWER'S NAME	ROOM
Dec. 7	Becca Prather	203
March 5	Kassie St.Clair	104
April 9	Katie Hovet	206

E		
W		
Author	Ward	
Title	The Biggest Bear	

DATE DUE	BORROWER'S NAME	ROOM

I'M A GOOD LIBRARY CITIZEN

I have clean hands
when I read a book.

I always carry my books to
and from school in a book bag.

I never write, scribble, draw,
glue, or cut the pages of a
library book.

I keep my books safe at home
from water, pets, and little
brothers and sisters.

I mark my place in a
book with a bookmark.
I never fold the pages.

Grilled Cheese.

I turn the page of a book
using the top corner.

I always remember to return
my library books on time!

Color and bring home to display.

BOOK CARE RULES
BOOKMARKS

Reproduce and use as incentives.

DO... Treat me with respect. Keep me safe in a book bag!

DO... Have clean hands when you are reading me!

DO... Return me on time to the library!

DO... Keep me safe at home from little sisters, brothers, water and animals.

WHAT IS AN AUTHOR?

Explain to the children the definition of an "author." An author is someone who writes the words that we read in books.

Show the children different books and point out the name of the author on the cover, the spine, and on the title page of the book.

Reproduce the book. Ask the children to be the author and write the words that should go with the pictures.

WHAT IS AN ILLUSTRATOR?

Explain to the children the definition of an "illustrator." An illustrator is someone who creates the pictures that we see in books.

Show the children different books and point out the name of the illustrator on the cover, the spine, and on the title page of the book.

Reproduce the book. Ask the children to be the illustrator and create the pictures that should go with the words.

Leo, the Library Mouse likes to read books.

Leo has many books.

WORKING TOGETHER AS AN AUTHOR/ILLUSTRATOR TEAM

Reproduce this page. Have the children work in teams as an author and an illustrator. One child writes the words and the other child illustrates the pictures.

fold #1

fold #2

4. 3.

1. 2.

Illustrated by: _____

Written by: _____

A TITLE HELPS YOU FIND THE RIGHT BOOK

Young children need to be taught how to look for books. Take some time and discuss book titles with your first graders.

GUESS WHAT THE BOOK IS ABOUT
Show the children a book and read its title to the class. Ask the children what they think the book will be about. Repeat this with several books.

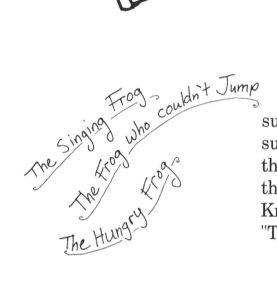

MAKING UP BOOK TITLES
Another fun activity is to give the children a subject and have them think of titles for that subject. For example: If you gave the children the subject, "airplanes." The children might think of titles such as "Everything I Want To Know About Airplanes," "The Biggest Airplane." "The Airplane Who Was Afraid To Fly," etc.

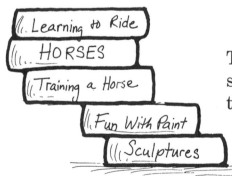

SORTING BOOKS BY TITLE
Fill a large tabletop with a variety of books. The books should cover two or three different subjects (i.e. Halloween, pets, and trains). Have the children sort the books by their subject.

This is the first step in learning how to use the library as a research or reference tool. Young children will begin to learn that they can find information in the library.

CAN YOU FIND THE RIGHT BOOK?

You need a book. Look at what you need. Then color the correct book.

HAT

The Bat
Book

The Rat
Book

The
Big Hat
Book

TOP

The Box

The
Red Top

The Fox

SUN

Red Sun
Book

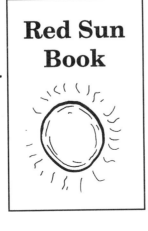

Run, Run
Book

Fun Book

CAN YOU FIND THE RIGHT BOOK?

You need a book. Look at what you need. Then color the correct book.

CATS

Bats, Bats Book

Big Cats Book

Hats, Hats Book

BEES

Big Bees Book

The See Book

ME!

The Me Book

PINS

The Win Book

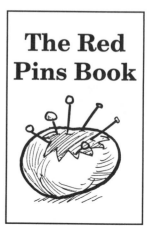
The Tin Book

The Red Pins Book

TITLE PAGE

The first page of a book is called the *title page*. It tells you the title of the book and the name of the author.

On a blackboard draw the example below and ask the children the following questions.

```
┌─────────────────────────┐
│                         │
│      The Sun            │
│                         │
│        by               │
│      Jan Red            │
│                         │
└─────────────────────────┘
```

The title page tells you the name of the title.
What is the title? The Sun

The title page tells you the name of the author.
Who is the author? Jan Red

• Show the children a variety of books and the title pages. Ask the children to locate the title of the book and the name of the author.

THE TITLE PAGE   Read the page.
Answer the questions.

```
+---------------------------------+
|                                 |
|                                 |
|    THE BOX                      |
|                                 |
|         by                      |
|                                 |
|    Jan Top                      |
|                                 |
+---------------------------------+
```

1.   Who wrote the book?   _____

2.   What is the title of the book?   _____

THE TITLE PAGE   Read the page.
Answer the questions.

The Bat

by

Rob Web

1. Who wrote the book? _____

2. What is the title of the book? _____

THE TITLE PAGE   Read the page.
Answer the questions.

THE
CAT

by
Lin Kar

1.   Who wrote the book?   _____

2.   What is the title of the book?   _____

TABLE PAGE

The second page of a book is the *table page*. This is the page that helps people find things in a book.

On a blackboard draw the example below and ask the children the following questions.

Bats.. page 1

Cats.. page 5

Bees .... page 6

Where can you find bats?

It is found on page 1.

Where can you find cats?

It is found on page 5.

Where can you find bees?

It is found on page 6.

TABLE PAGE

Read the table.
Answer the questions.

Table Page

Dogs .... page 2

Cats .... page 4

Bees .... page 6

Dogs are on page?   _____.

Bees are on page?   _____.

Cats are on page?   _____.

TABLE PAGE

Read the table.
Answer the questions.

Table Page

Hats .... page 3

Cars .... page 5

Tops .... page 7

Hats are on page? _____.

Tops are on page? _____.

Cars are on page? _____.

TABLE PAGE

Read the table.
Answer the questions.

Table Page

Bats .... page 1

Cats .... page 3

Rats .... page 5

Rats are on page?   _____.

Bats are on page?   _____.

Cats are on page?   _____.

PICTURE PAGE

The *picture page* tells about the pictures and where they can be located in the book.

On a blackboard draw the example below and ask the children to answer the following questions.

Cat, black .... page 3

Cat, brown .... page 5

Cat, white... page 9

Where can you find a picture of a black cat?

It is on page <u>3.</u>

Where can you find a picture of a brown cat?

It is on page <u>5.</u>

Where can you find a picture of a white cat?

It is on page <u>9.</u>

PICTURE PAGE

Read the page.
Answer the questions.

BOX

Box, big............................... page 2

Box, red .... page 4

Box, tall .... page 6

The big box is on page?   _____

The red box is on page?   _____

The tall box is on page?   _____

PICTURE PAGE

Read the page.
Answer the questions.

HATS

Tall hats .... page 5

Red hats .... page 7

Big hats .... page 9

The big hats are on page? _____

The tall hats are on page? _____

The red hats are on page? _____

DIFFERENT KINDS OF BOOKS FICTION/NONFICTION

The library in your school has many kinds of books. One kind of book is a story book. Story books often have make-believe stories. Make-believe stories or stories that are about things that are not real are called **fiction** books. Books that tell you about real things or facts are called **nonfiction** books.

On a blackboard draw the example below and ask the children to answer the following questions.

The Story of Three Talking Mice

All About Mice

Which book tells about real things?
> *All About Mice* tells about real mice. This is a **nonfiction** book.

Now look at *The Story of Three Talking Mice*. This story is not real. Mice cannot talk.
> *The Story of Three Talking Mice* is a **fiction** book.

Show the children titles of books that provide clear examples of fiction and nonfiction. Here are some examples:
- A book about rocks & *Sylvester and the Magic Pebble.*
- A book about rabbits & *The Velveteen Rabbit.*
- A book about living on a farm & *Charlotte's Web.*
- A book about weather & *The Snowy Day.*
- A book about cooking & *Stone Soup.*

FICTION OR NONFICTION

Look at the two books. Color the **fiction** book.

LEARN ABOUT REAL MICE

Leo the Library Mouse!

WHICH IS A FICTION BOOK?

Read the book titles. Color the fiction books.

The Story of Brown Bear

ALL ABOUT BEARS

THE TREE BOOK

The Little Tree That Could Sing

The Car Book

THE MAGIC CAR

WHICH IS A FICTION BOOK?

Read the book titles. Color the fiction books.

Three Naughty Mice

ALL ABOUT MICE

The Spider Book

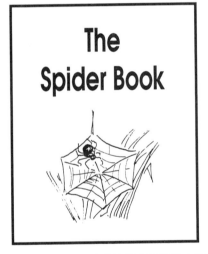

The Magical Web

Learn About Frogs

SAM, THE PURPLE FROG

FICTION OR NONFICTION

NAME _____

Look at the two books. Color the **nonfiction** book.

THE MAGIC FLOWER

PLANTING FLOWERS

WHICH IS A NONFICTION BOOK?

Read the titles. Color the nonfiction books.

The Polk-A-Dot Fish Story

The Fish Book

All About Insects

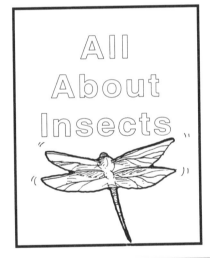

The Unhappy Ladybug

The Dog Book

THE STORY OF THE GIANT PUPPY

WHICH IS A NONFICTION BOOK?

Read the titles. Color the nonfiction books.

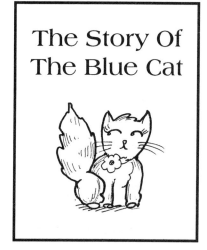

DRAW THE COVER
OF YOUR FAVORITE BOOK
The cover of a book protects the pages of the book.

NAME _____

PRINT THE TITLE OF YOUR FAVORITE STORY ON THE SPINE OF THE BOOK

The spine helps hold the pages of the book together.

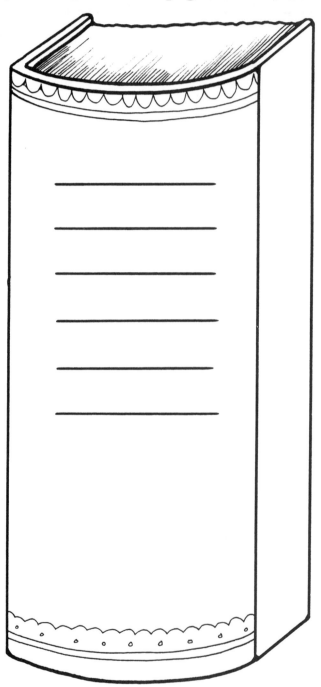

NAME _____

REVIEW LIBRARY WORDS

Draw a line from the word to the correct picture.

author

illustrator

book

spine

cover

title page

library

fiction

nonfiction

NAME _____

READING INCENTIVE CHARTS

Reproduce these charts for the first graders. Each time a book is read the child may mark or place a sticker on his or her chart.

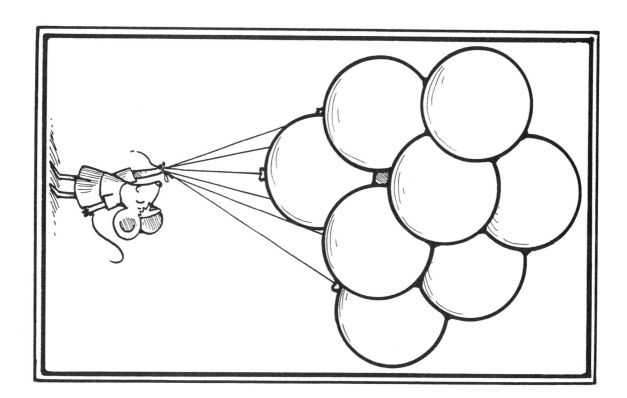

GRADE TWO

By second grade children are rapidly learning how to read! This new skill creates a new interest in the library and in all the new books available to them.

Librarians will need to assist these children in becoming more knowledgeable in locating fiction books in the library, using call numbers, and in understanding different parts of a book.

CONTENTS

BOOK CARE REVIEW

Look at the picture and write the book care rule.

_____

- - - - - - - - - - - - - - - - -

_____

- - - - - - - - - - - - - - - - -

_____

_____

- - - - - - - - - - - - - - - - -

_____

- - - - - - - - - - - - - - - - -

_____

_____

- - - - - - - - - - - - - - - - -

_____

- - - - - - - - - - - - - - - - -

_____

_____

- - - - - - - - - - - - - - - - -

_____

- - - - - - - - - - - - - - - - -

_____

BOOKMARKS FOR GOOD LIBRARY CITIZENSHIP

I
RETURN
MY
LIBRARY
BOOKS
ON
TIME

I Use A
Bookmark
To Mark
My Place
In A Book

Carry
Books In
A Book
Bag To
And From
School

I HELP
KEEP
BOOKS
STRAIGHT
ON THE
BOOK
SHELVES

BORROWING A BOOK FROM THE LIBRARY

The library has many books. Your school has a school library where you are welcome to visit and check out books. When you check out a book it is called **borrowing** a book. This means that you can take the book home, but you must remember to bring the book back to the library.

How do you borrow a book? First, find a book. Then take it to the library desk. The librarian will stamp the book. The stamp tells you when to bring the book back to the library. Then write your name on the library card.

When you sign your name on the library card, remember to use the first line on the card. You can practice on this card.

E		
F		

Author	Flora	

Title	Kassie Wins The Game	

DATE DUE	BORROWER'S NAME	ROOM

DATE DUE	BORROWER'S NAME	ROOM

PARTS OF A BOOK REVIEW

Look at the picture and write the book care rule.

WORD BANK

Spine   Cover   Title

Author   Publisher

USING BOOKS — THE TITLE PAGE

You can learn much from books. Books have many parts. Each part of a book can help you.

The first page of a book is called the *title page*. The title page can help you. The title of the book is on the title page, along with the author's name, and the name of the publisher. If the book has pictures in it, you may see the name of the person who created those pictures on the title page. This person is called the illustrator.

Here is a list of vocabulary words for you to remember:

The name of the book is called the *title*.

The person who wrote the book is called the *author*.

The company that puts the books together is called the *publisher* (sometimes publishers are also called presses).

The person who makes the pictures for the books is called the *illustrator*.

• Show the children examples of titles in real books. Have them practice reading this information.

• Have the children design their own title page of a book, by making up their own title, author, illustrator and publisher. Let the children share their designs with the rest of the class.

```
┌─────────────────────────────────┐
│                                 │
│   The Brown Bear                │
│                                 │
│           by                    │
│       Mary Brook                │
│     Illustrated by              │
│       Karen Cub                 │
│                                 │
│       River Press               │
│                                 │
└─────────────────────────────────┘
```

Write the above example on the blackboard and ask the children the following questions.

What is the title of the story?	The title is The Brown Bear.
What is the book about?	It is about a brown bear.
Who is the author?	The author is Mary Brook.
Who is the illustrator?	The illustrator is Karen Cub.
Who is the publisher?	The publisher is River Press.

Answer these questions.

The Green Spider

by
Ted Web

Lace Press

1.   What is the title of this book? _____

_____

2.   Who is the author? _____

3.   What is the subject of this book?

_____

NAME _____

Answer these questions.

The Brown Bat

by
Joe Smith

Fly Publishers

1. What is the title of this book? _____

_____

2. Who is the author? _____

3. What is the subject of this book?

_____

NAME _____

Answer these questions.

The Orange Egg

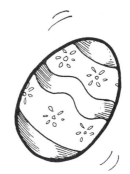

by
Ted Grass

**Illustrated by
Bob Rabbit**

Eggtime Press

1. What is the title of this book? _____

   _____

2. Who is the author? _____

3. Who is the publisher of this book?

   _____

Answer these questions.

THE PURPLE TREE

by
May Leaf

Illustrated by
John Trunk

Seed Publishers, Inc.

1. What is the title of this book? _____

    _____

2. Who is the author? _____

3. Who is the illustrator? _____

4. What is the subject? _____

NAME _____

Answer these questions.

The Sky Book

**by
June Star**

**Illustrated by
Cammy Comet**

Star Press

1. What is the title of this book? _____

    _____

2. Who is the author? _____

3. Who is the publisher? _____

4. What is the subject of this book?

    _____

NAME _____

Answer these questions.

# The Snow Book

by
Peter Winter

Illustrated by
Fran Flake

Cold Publishers, Inc.

1.   What is the title of this book? _____

_____

2.   Who is the author? _____

3.   Who is the illustrator? _____

4.   Who is the publisher? _____

_____

5.   What is the subject of this book? _____

THE TITLE PAGE & THE COPYRIGHT PAGE

You have learned about the information on the title page. Now take a look at the copyright page. The copyright page tells you what year the book was made, who made the book, and where the book was made.

The Green Bird **By** **Mary Song** **String Press**	**String Press** **New Jersey** **©1993**

1. What is the title of this book? _____

2. Who is the author? _____

3. Where was the book made? _____

4. Who made the book? _____

5. Could you read about puppies in this book? _____

6. Could you read about parrots in this book? _____

7. Could you learn about stars in this book? _____

THE TITLE PAGE &
THE COPYRIGHT PAGE

You have learned about the information on the title page. Now take a look at the copyright page. The copyright page tells you what year the book was made, who made the book, and where the book was made.

Puppy, Puppy **by** **Peter Bark** **Woof Publishers**	**Woof Publishers** **New York** **©1993**

1. What is the title of this book? _____

2. Who is the author? _____

3. Where was the book made? _____

4. Who made the book? _____

5. Could you read about puppies in this book? _____

6. Could you read about parrots in this book? _____

7. Could you learn about stars in this book? _____

TABLE OF CONTENTS

How can you find out what a book is about? You can look at the second page of a book. It is called the *Table of Contents*. The Table of Contents tells where you will find the beginning page of each chapter. Below is a table of contents for the teacher to recreate on the blackboard. Ask the children the following questions, and help them to learn how this page can be useful when looking up information in a book.

Chapter 1 — Bees Buzz	**Page 1**
Chapter 2 — Bugs and Flowers	**Page 4**
Chapter 3 — Cats and Food	**Page 6**
Chapter 4 — Dogs as Pets	**Page 7**

Can you find chapter 1? What is it about?
Chapter 1 is about <u>Bees Buzz</u>. It is on <u>page 1.</u>

Can you find chapter 2? What is it about?
Chapter 2 is about <u>Bugs and Flowers</u>. It is on <u>page 4.</u>

Can you find chapter 3? What is it about?
Chapter 3 is about <u>Cats and Food</u>. It is on <u>page 6.</u>

Can you find chapter 4? What is it about?
Chapter 4 is about <u>Dogs as Pets</u>. It is on <u>page 7.</u>

NAME _____

TABLE OF CONTENTS

Use the Table of Contents to answer the questions.

BIRDS

Chapter 1   **Nests**

Chapter 2   **Kinds of Birds**

Chapter 3   **Eggs**

Chapter 4   **Colors**

Chapter 5   **Songs**

1.   Where can you find eggs? _____

2.   What chapter is about colors? _____

3.   Chapter 1 is called? _____

4.   Kinds of Birds is chapter _____ .

5.   Chapter 5 is called? _____

TABLE OF CONTENTS

Use the Table of Contents to answer the questions.

FLOWERS

Chapter 1	**Kinds of Flowers**
Chapter 2	**Tall Flowers**
Chapter 3	**Seeds**
Chapter 4	**How to Grow Flowers**
Chapter 5	**How to Cut Flowers**

---

1. What is chapter 1 about? _____

2. What is chapter 2 about? _____

3. Seeds are in chapter _____ .

4. How to Grow Flowers is chapter _____ .

5. How to Cut Flowers is chapter _____ .

TABLE OF CONTENTS

Use the Table of Contents to answer the questions.

TRAVEL

Chapter 1   Planes

Chapter 2   Trucks

Chapter 3   Cars

Chapter 4   Boats

Chapter 5   Buses

1. What is chapter 4 about? _____

2. What is chapter 1 about? _____

3. Trucks is chapter _____ .

4. What is chapter 5 about? _____

5. Cars is in chapter _____ .

NAME _____

TABLE OF CONTENTS

Use the Table of Contents to answer the questions.

<table>
<tr><td>Chapter 1 — Bees Buzz</td><td>Page 1</td></tr>
<tr><td>Chapter 2 — Seeds</td><td>Page 3</td></tr>
<tr><td>Chapter 3 — Trees</td><td>Page 7</td></tr>
<tr><td>Chapter 4 — Vegetable Plants</td><td>Page 10</td></tr>
<tr><td>Chapter 5 — Roots</td><td>Page 12</td></tr>
<tr><td>Chapter 6 — Stems</td><td>Page 15</td></tr>
<tr><td>Chapter 7 — How To Buy Flowers</td><td>Page 18</td></tr>
<tr><td>Chapter 8 — How To Plant Flowers</td><td>Page 20</td></tr>
<tr><td>Chapter 9 — When To Plant Flowers</td><td>Page 25</td></tr>
</table>

1. On what page can you find out about seeds? _____

2. You can find roots on page _____

3. Vegetable Plants begins on page? _____

4. Stems begins on page? _____

5. What is the last chapter in the book? _____

   _____

6. What chapter starts on page 7? _____

7. What chapter starts on page 3? _____

8. What is the first chapter in the book? _____

   _____

9. How many pages in chapter 1? _____

10. How many chapters in the book? _____

11. Is there a chapter about wildflowers? _____

12. Is there a chapter about sunflowers? _____

13. Could you learn how to buy flowers in this book? ___

TABLE OF CONTENTS

Use the Table of Contents to answer the questions.

1. On what page can you find out about cars? _____

2. You can find submarines on what page? _____

3. The chapter on spaceships begins on what page?____

4. What is the first chapter about? _____

5. What chapter starts on page 20? _____

6. What chapter starts on page 7? _____

7. What is the last chapter of the book? _____

8. How many pages in chapter 1? _____

9. How many chapters in the book? _____

10. What is chapter 3 about?_____

11. Is there a chapter about speedboats? _____

12. Is there a chapter about rowboats? _____

13. Could you use this table of contents to find out about
    kites? _____

BOOK INDEX

In some books there are many different subjects. You can find these subjects by looking in the back of the book at the book index.

The subjects are listed in alphabetical order.

Let's say that you have a list of subjects about bees, bugs, cats, and dogs. The list would look like this:

bees	page 3
bugs	page 7
cats	page 10
dogs	page 15

NAME _____

BOOK INDEX

Use the book index to answer the questions.

BIRDS

Birds, colors	**page 2**
Birds, kinds	**page 3**
Eggs, size	**page 4**
Eggs, colors	**page 5**
Nests, big	**page 8**
Nests, small	**page 10**

1. Where can you find out about the color of birds?

   _____

2. Where can you find small nests? _____

3. Where can you find out about the colors of eggs?

   _____

4. What is on page 4? _____

5. What is on page 3? _____

BOOK INDEX

Use the book index to answer the questions.

FLOWERS

Flowers, cutting	**page 1**
Flowers, growing	**page 3**
Flowers, planting	**page 7**
Flowers, seeds	**page 8**
Flowers, short	**page 10**
Flowers, tall	**page 12**

1. Tall flowers are on page? _____

2. Short flowers are on page? _____

3. Seeds are on page? _____

4. Where can you find how to grow flowers? _____

5. Where can you find how to cut flowers? _____

NAME _____

BOOK INDEX

Use the book index to answer the questions.

TRAVEL

Boats, small	**page 1**
Boats, speed	**page 2**
Buses, city	**page 3**
Cars, big	**page 6**
Cars, small	**page 8**
Planes, airports	**page 9**
Trucks, big	**page 10**

1. Small cars are on page? _____

2. Planes are on page? _____

3. Big trucks are on page? _____

4. Speed boats are on page? _____

5. Sailboats are on page? _____

BOOK INDEX

Use the book index to answer the questions.

VEGETABLES

Beans	**page 2**
Broccoli	**page 3**
Carrots	**page 5**
Eggplant	**page 7**
Peas	**page 9**
Potatoes	**page 11**
Turnips	**page 16**
Wax beans	**page 21**

1. On what page are the carrots? _____

2. Is the yam in the index? _____

3. On what page are the turnips? _____

4. Are snap beans in this index? _____

5. What is the last vegetable in the index? _____

6. What is the first vegetable in the index? _____

7. Wax beans are on what page? _____

8. How many vegetables are in this index? _____

9. Is eggplant in this index? _____

10. Is broccoli in this index? _____

11. You are writing a report about spinach. Is spinach
    listed in the index? _____

12. You are writing a report about carrots and peas. What
    pages will help you? _____

13. You are writing a report about potatoes, peas, and
    beans. What pages will help you?_____

THE ILLUSTRATION PAGE

The illustration page is similar to the contents page and the index page. You can use it to look up information. You can locate where the pictures are in a book by using the illustration page. Use the sample illustration page to answer the questions.

SPACE

Earth	**page 3**
Mars	**page 4**
Milky Way	**page 20**
Moon	**page 1**
Night Sky	**page 21**
Pluto	**page 13**
Space Clothes	**page 7**
Space Rockets	**page 10**
Stars at Night	**page 8**
Sun	**page 6**

1. On what page can you find the moon? _____
2. On what page can you find Mars? _____
3. Space clothes are on what page? _____
4. The night sky is on what page? _____
5. What will you find on page 13? _____
6. What will you find on page 8? _____
7. The Milky Way is on what page? _____
8. The sun is on what page? _____
9. How many illustrations are in this book? _____
10. What two illustrations tell you about stars? _____
11. Can you find an illustration about Neptune? _____
12. Can you find an illustration about Pluto? _____

THE ILLUSTRATION PAGE

The illustration page is similar to the contents page and the index page. You can use it to look up information. You can locate where the pictures are in a book by using the illustration page. Use the sample illustration page to answer the questions.

PLANTING

Cutting Flowers	**page 1**
Digging in Your Garden	**page 11**
Finding the Right Seeds	**page 10**
Finding the Right Trees	**page 3**
Finding the Right Vegetable Plants	**page 13**
Gardens of the World	**page 5**
How to Plant a Garden	**page 4**
Insects and Flowers	**page 7**
Purple and Blue Flower Gardens	**page 9**
Yellow and Red Flower Gardens	**page 6**

---

1. On what page are insects and flowers? _____

2. Gardens of the world are found on what page? _____

3. What will you find on page 11? _____

4. What will you find on page 4? _____

5. The yellow and red flower gardens are on page _____ .

6. The picture of vegetable plants is on page _____ .

7. The picture of trees is on what page? _____

8. Can you find an illustration of purple flowers? _____

9. Can you find an illustration of a garden hose? _____

10. Can you find an illustration of seeds? _____

11. What will you find on page 9? _____

KINDS OF BOOKS
FICTION & NONFICTION

There are two kinds of books in the library. One kind of book is called a **fiction** book. Fiction books are story books that are make-believe or imaginary stories. These kinds of stories are not real; they are pretend. Books that tell you about real things or give you facts or information are called **nonfiction** books.

• Show the children books that will provide them with clear examples of the difference between fiction and nonfiction.

• Have a scavenger hunt in the library. Divide the class into two groups. Everyone in group one should choose a fiction book from the book shelves. Everyone in group two should choose a nonfiction book. The group that has made the most accurate choices is the winner.

• Have the children make up titles of books. These titles should either reflect a fiction book or a nonfiction book.

• On a table in the center of your library, stack a multitude of fiction and nonfiction books. Let the children sort the books into fiction and nonfiction categories.

FINDING A FICTION AND A NONFICTION BOOK

Choose one fiction book and one nonfiction book from the shelves in the library. Draw the covers of each book. Label the fiction book with the word "fiction." Label the nonfiction book with the word "nonfiction."

MAKE A LIST OF
FICTION AND NONFICTION

NAME _____

Make a list of fiction books and a list of nonfiction books. Search through the library and copy down the titles of the books in the appropriate column.

FICTION

NONFICTION

PUTTING FICTION CALL NUMBERS IN ORDER

Library books are kept on the shelves in alphabetical order. When you look at the spine of a book you will find letters on the spine. These letters are the first two letters of the author's last name and are called **call numbers.**

Here is an example. If you saw a book written by a person named Peter **Br**ook, you would find the letter "B" and the letter "r."

Br

Let's look at the call number for the author Jane **Pa**ge. The letter "P" and the letter "a" make the call number.

Pa

Let's make another call number. The titles of the book is Purple Bugs. The author is Jane Tree. How do you write a call number? Look at the author's name. The author is Jane Tree. What is the first letter of her last name? What is the second letter of her last name. The call number would be "Tr."

Tr

Sometimes you will see the capital letter "E." Then the call number looks like this.
The capital letter "E" means the book is an easy book. This will help you look for books in the library too.

| E |
| Tr |

WRITE THE CALL NUMBERS

1. Peter Star
   The call number is

2. Sally Bookmark
   The call number is

3. June Page
   The call number is

4. Joe Read
   The call number is

5. Happy Spine
   The call number is

WRITE THE CALL NUMBERS

1. John Sky
   The call number is

2. Sally Sun
   The call number is

3. Lou Star
   The call number is

4. April Long
   The call number is

5. May Book
   The call number is

WRITE THE CALL NUMBERS

1. Jane Stone
   The call number is

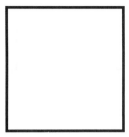

2. Peter Paper
   The call number is

3. Robert Hall
   The call number is

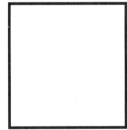

4. Rose Apple
   The call number is

5. Sue Bee
   The call number is

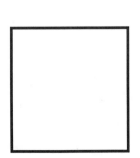

ARRANGE THE FICTION BOOKS

Look at the call numbers. Print them on the spines of the books in alphabetical order.

Qu   Br   Tu   Mo   An

Cr   No   Re   Or   Hi

ARRANGE THE FICTION BOOKS

When the first letters are the same, you need to look at the second letter of the author's name. For example: Ba, Be, Br would be in alphabetical order. Put the following groups of call numbers in alpabetical order.

Ba   St   Br

Al   Ab   Ba

Kr   Re   Rk

NONFICTIONS BOOKS AND THEIR CALL NUMBERS

A call number is found on the spine of the book. It tells you where you can find a book in the library. You have learned that fiction books are put on the shelves according to the first two letters of the author's last name. When you put nonfiction books on the shelves they are also organized by the first two letters of the author's last name, but they also are organized with numbers.

There are ten sections of the library. Each section holds a certain kind of book. Each section has it's own numbers. *(On the following page is a chart that may be reproduced for the children to use with the activities in this section of the book.)*

When you organize nonfiction books in the library, you must first put the numbers in order. After the numbers have been put in order, then you can put the letters in alphabetical order.

For example: If you were given the call numbers of:

523	546	599	546
Ta	Br	We	Ba

You would first put the numbers in order:
523
546
546
599

Next, you would look at the letters, and the correct order would be:
523 Ta
546 Ba
546 Br
599 We

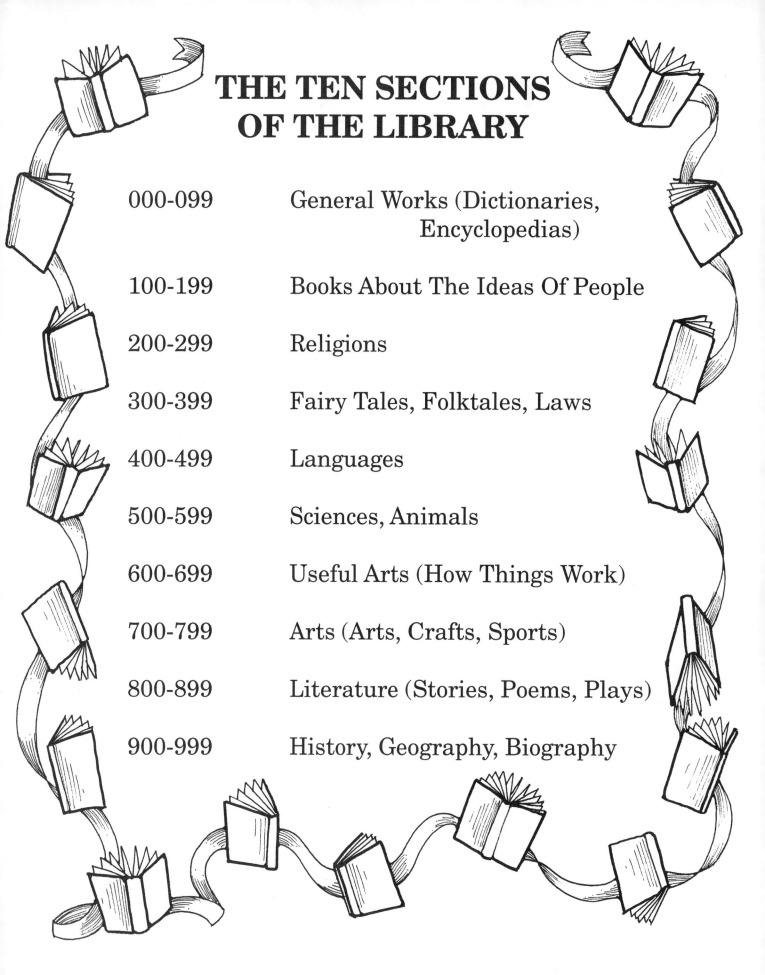

THE TEN SECTIONS OF THE LIBRARY

000-099	General Works (Dictionaries, Encyclopedias)
100-199	Books About The Ideas Of People
200-299	Religions
300-399	Fairy Tales, Folktales, Laws
400-499	Languages
500-599	Sciences, Animals
600-699	Useful Arts (How Things Work)
700-799	Arts (Arts, Crafts, Sports)
800-899	Literature (Stories, Poems, Plays)
900-999	History, Geography, Biography

SEARCHING THROUGH THE NONFICTION SECTION OF THE LIBRARY

Use the chart on page 102. Write the number of the section of the library where you would find these books.

1. Book of Poems _____

2. History of New Jersey _____

3. Baseball _____

4. Bears _____

5. Book of Laws _____

6. Animals and Plants _____

7. Book of Plays _____

8. Cinderella _____

9. Learning French _____

10. Building Machines _____

11. Rocks _____

12. Geography of the U.S.A. _____

SEARCHING THROUGH THE NONFICTION SECTION OF THE LIBRARY

Use the chart on page 102. Write the number of the section of the library where you would find these books.

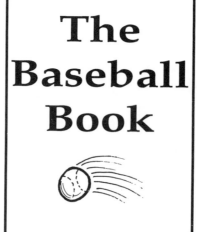

SEARCHING THROUGH THE NONFICTION SECTION OF THE LIBRARY

Use the chart on page 102. Write the number of the section of the library where you would find these books.

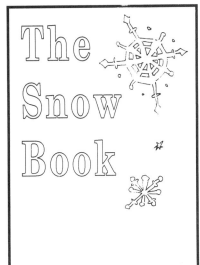

_____

_____

_____

_____

_____

_____

SEARCHING THROUGH THE NONFICTION SECTION OF THE LIBRARY

Use the chart on page 102. Write the number of the section of the library where you would find these books.

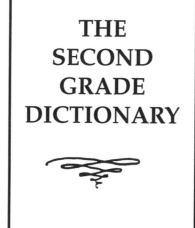

PUTTING NONFICTION CALL NUMBERS IN ORDER

Look at each group of numbers. Put them in numerical order.

1. 470   480   450   420   430

    ___   ___   ___   ___   ___

2. 850   890   860   830   820

    ___   ___   ___   ___   ___

3. 670   680   630   620   610

    ___   ___   ___   ___   ___

4. 537   536   534   535   533

    ___   ___   ___   ___   ___

5. 963   969   968   965   975

    ___   ___   ___   ___   ___

NONFICTION CALL NUMBERS

Ordering nonfiction call numbers is a difficult task for a second grade child. Take it slow and provide many examples for the children to see. Here are some examples that can be demonstrated on a blackboard.

Let's look at three call numbers.
975 Ab
974 Ab
973 Ab

Which comes first? Answer:
973 Ab
974 Ab
975 Ab

Let's look at three more call numbers:
965 Ab
934 Ab
923 Ab

Which comes first? Answer:
923 Ab
934 Ab
965 Ab

Let's look at three more call numbers.
865 Ab
934 Ab
323 Ab

Which comes first? Answer:
323 Ab
865 Ab
934 Ab

Let's look at three more call numbers.
865 Ho
934 Ho
322 Bo

Which comes first? Answer:
322 Bo
865 Ho
934 Ho

Let's look at three more call numbers.
865 Ab
934 Ho
323 Ta

Which comes first? Answer:
323 Ta
865 Ab
934 Ho

PUTTING NONFICTION
CALL NUMBERS IN ORDER

565 _____   565 Ha _____

432 _____   432 Ho _____

152 _____   152 Hc _____

384 _____   384 Hi _____

974 _____   974 Ho _____

897 Ab _____   575 Ba _____

384 Za _____   431 Bo _____

270 Ho _____   770 Ho _____

350 Ti _____   652 Ca _____

487 Ta _____   432 Da _____

PUTTING NONFICTION CALL NUMBERS IN ORDER

261 _____   261 Bu _____

175 _____   175 Bo _____

380 _____   380 Bi _____

490 _____   490 Be _____

600 _____   600 Ba _____

374 To _____   490 Ba _____

291 To _____   870 Ta _____

634 Bo _____   491 Zo _____

504 Ho _____   406 Hi _____

190 Ro _____   230 Ho _____

PUTTING NONFICTION
CALL NUMBERS IN ORDER

244 _____   204 Hu _____

544 _____   406 Ro _____

600 _____   509 Ti _____

240 _____   809 Re _____

902 _____   309 Ra _____

344 Ha _____   707 Ru _____

544 Ho _____   609 Ro _____

600 He _____   703 Si _____

240 Hi _____   709 Tc _____

902 Hy _____   230 Ma _____

LIBRARY SUBJECTS

The library puts books in order. This order is by subject. A subject is what the book is about. *The Book of Cats* is about cats. *The Book of Puppies* is about puppies. These books are about pets. You will find them in the same place in your library.

The library has a card for each book that is in the library. These cards are put in A-B-C order. This order helps you find books. There are three cards for each book that is in the library. They are called

SUBJECT CARD
– what the book is about

AUTHOR CARD
– who wrote the book

TITLE CARD
– the name of the book

You have three ways to find books in the library. The subject card is always in capital letters.

LIBRARY SUBJECTS
Look at this subject card.

BOATS

Brown, Tom. <u>The Story of Boats</u>

---

1. What word is in capital letters? _____

2. Who is the author? _____

3. What is the title? _____

4. What is this book about? _____

SUBJECT CARDS

Write the example below on the blackboard. Discuss the card with the children and ask them the questions at the bottom of the page.

DOGS (subject)

Fur, Kate. (author)

<u>Life of a Dog.</u> (title)

The subject is in capital letters.

(DOGS)

The author's name is written with the last name first.

(Fur, Kate)

The title is underlined.

(<u>The Life of a Dog.</u>)

PUTTING SUBJECT CARDS IN ORDER

At the bottom of the page, write the subjects in ABC order.

BATS
Brown, Lin. Bats in Trees.

BOATS
Brown, Tom.
The Story of Boats.

BEES
Buzz, Jane.
Do You Know About Bees?

---

1. _____

2. _____

3. _____

PUTTING SUBJECT CARDS IN ORDER

Look at each group of subjects. Can you put them in library order?

FLOWERS _____

ROCKS _____

TREES _____

BLACKBIRD _____

CROW _____

RED BIRD _____

FISH _____

RABBITS _____

BIRDS _____

CATS _____

DOGS _____

MICE _____

KITES _____

TOPS _____

BIKES _____

WHICH SUBJECT?

When you visit the library, you will see many subjects.
Use the subject bank and find the large subject for each group.

```
+------------------------------------------------------+
|                    SUBJECT BANK                      |
|                                                      |
|   PETS      FOOD      SPORTS      ANIMALS             |
+------------------------------------------------------+
```

BASKETBALL

FOOTBALL

SOCCER

_____

APPLE

BREAD

BUTTER

_____

DOG

CAT

FISH

_____

BEAR

TIGER

LION

_____

NAME _____

WRITE YOUR OWN SUBJECT LIST
Write a list for each subject.

PETS

1. _____

2. _____

3. _____

TREES

1. _____

2. _____

3. _____

CLOTHES

1. _____

2. _____

3. _____

FOOD

1. _____

2. _____

3. _____

NAME _____

WRITE YOUR OWN SUBJECT CARD

_____ subject

_____ author

_____ title

1. Write your subject. _____

2. Write your author. _____

3. Write your title. _____

MATCHING BOOK TITLES TO SUBJECTS

Find the card that matches the book title.
Write the title under the card.

1. **The Red Bird Book**
2. **Pets and You**
3. **Dogs and Puppies**

BIRDS
Wing, Ted.
The Red Bird Book.

PETS
Vet, Jane.
Pets and You.

DOGS
Paw, Lin.
Dogs and Puppies.

WHERE ARE SUBJECT CARDS FOUND?

Subject cards are put in the same place. They are put in alphabetical order. It is easy to use subject cards. They can all be found in a drawer called the card *catalog drawer.* All the subject cards are kept in the *subject catalog drawer.*

Write the following example on the blackboard and ask the children if they can you find all the subjects in this catalog drawer?

B
Subject Catalog Drawer

BUTTERFLIES
TREES
BOATS
BEES
SKY

Which ones do not belong in this drawer?

MATCHING SUBJECTS TO THE
CORRECT CATALOG DRAWER

Put the subjects under the correct drawer.

CATS	AIRPLANE	COLORS
BATS	BEES	BIKES
APPLES	COOKIES	ALLIGATORS

A	B	C

_____   _____   _____

_____   _____   _____

_____   _____   _____

SECOND GRADE LIBRARY AWARDS

1. _____

2. _____

3. _____

4. _____

5. _____

_____ is a GREAT illustrator

I KNOW HOW TO **INVESTIGATE** THE LIBRARY!

MY FAVORITE BOOKS

SUGGESTED AUTHORS FOR KINDERGARTEN, FIRST GRADE AND SECOND GRADE CHILDREN

There are many wonderful authors from which to select. Here is a list to get you started and one that you can keep adding on to.

1. Aliki
2. Alexander, Martha
3. Allard, Harry
4. Bemelmans, Ludwig
5. Berenstain, Stan and Jan
6. Burton, Virginia Lee
7. Brandenberg, Franz
8. Bridwell, Norman
9. Brown, Margaret Wise
10. Brown, Marc
11. Carle, Eric
12. Cazet, Denys
13. Crews, Donald
14. De Brunhoff, Jean and Laurent
15. De Paola, Tomie
16. Ehlert, Lois
17. Freeman, Don
18. Gackenback, Dick
19. Galdone, Paul
20. Gantos, Jack
21. Hargreves, Roger
22. Hoban, Russel
23. Henkes, Kevin
24. Hutchins, Pat
25. Keats, Ezra Jack
26. Kellogg, Steven
27. Krauss, Pat
28. Krauss, Ruth
29. Kroll, Steven
30. Leonni, Leo
31. Lobel, Arnold
32. Marshall, James
33. Mayer, Mercer
34. McCloskey, Robert
35. McPhail, David
36. McKissack, Patricia
37. Minarik, Else Holmund
38. Munsch, Robert
39. Parish, Peggy
40. Peet, Bill
41. Pinkwater, Daniel
42. Rey, H.A.
43. Rockwell, Anne
44. Scarry, Richard
45. Sendak, Maurice
46. Sesame Street Golden Books
47. Seuss, Dr.
48. Stevenson, James
49. Titus, Eve
51. Troll First Start Easy Readers set of 41 - Grade One
52. Van Allsburg, Chris
53. Waber, Bernard
54. Wells, Rosemary
55. Williams, Vera B.
56. Wiseman, Bernard
57. Zion, Gene

GLOSSARY

1. *author*—A person who writes the words in a book.

2. *book pocket*—The book pocket is usually at the back of the book. It holds the library charge out card. And it will have the call number on it.

3. *book spine*—The book spine is the edge of a book. This is what you see when you pull a book from the shelves. You will find the call number on the spine.

4. *call number*—This number is on the spine of the book, book pocket, and library charge out card. It tells you where you can find a library book. Under the capital letter F, you will find the first two letters of the author's last name. The letter F stands for fiction.

5. *catalog card*— This card tells who wrote the book, the title of the book, publisher, copyright date, illustrations, and number of pages in the book.

6. *catalog card drawers*—The card catalog is made of catalog drawers. On the outside of each drawer are letters. These letters tell you the catalog cards in the drawer. For example, a drawer letters A–C has cards A, B, and C.

7. *copyright date*—This date is like the birth date of the book. It is the date the book was introduced to the public.

8. *fiction*—Fiction books tell you about people, places, or things. These stories are not true.

9. *illustration*—Illustrations are the pictures in the book.

10. *illustrator* — The person who creates (draws, paints, etc.) the pictures in a book.

11. **index**—An index is a list of subjects that are in the book. It is in alphabetical order. It is at the back of the book.

12. **library charge out card**—This card is in the library book pocket. It has the name of the book on it. The librarian holds this card until you return your book.

13. **magazine**—A magazine is a short collection of stories or articles. It usually appears once a month.

14. **nonfiction**—A nonfiction book tells a true story. The story is based upon facts. There are many kinds of nonfiction books.

15. **publisher**—The publisher is the group of people who make the book. They print it and put it together.

16. **table of contents**—A table of contents tells you the title of each chapter in the book. It is at the front of the book. A table of contents in the magazine tells you the names of the articles or stories in the magazine.

NOTES